PERDID

Chase Twichell lives in Princeton, New Jersey, where she is a lecturer in the University's Creative Writing Programme, and in the Adirondacks. Her two previous collections of poems are *Northern Spy* (1981) and *The Odds* (1986). She is married to the novelist Russell Banks.

Perdido

CHASE TWICHELL

faber and faber
LONDON · BOSTON

First published in the USA in 1991
by Farrar, Straus and Giroux, New York
and simultaneously in Canada by Harper Collins Canada Ltd

First published in Great Britain in 1992
by Faber and Faber Limited
3 Queen Square London WC1N 3AU

Printed in Great Britain by Clays Ltd, St Ives plc

A CIP record for this book is available from the British Library

ISBN 0–571–16564–8

2 4 6 8 10 9 7 5 3 1

Contents

ACKNOWLEDGMENTS

I'd like to thank the National Endowment for the Arts, the University of Alabama, and the New Jersey State Council on the Arts for grants which allowed me time to work on this book. Thanks also to the editors of the following magazines, where poems were first published, sometimes in earlier forms: Antaeus: *'Revenge.'* The Antioch Review: *'Worldliness.'* The Black Warrior Review: *'The Mistress' (as '400 ASA').* Chelsea: *'The Somersault.'* The Georgia Review: *'The Condom Tree'; 'Six Belons'; 'In the Exploded View.'* The Indiana Review: *'The Imaginary Land.'* The Iowa Review: *'Why All Good Music Is Sad'; 'Dream of the Interior'; 'Useless Islands'; 'Remember Death.'* New England Review/Bread Loaf Quarterly: *'A Minor Crush of Cells'; 'The Blade of Nostalgia'; 'One Physics'; 'The Cut.'* The Ohio Review: *'Chanel No. 5.'* The Ontario Review: *'O Miami.'* Poetry: *'Lapses of Turquoise Sea.'* The Seneca Review: *'A Whole Year of Love' (as 'The Other Knife'); 'Window in the Shape of a Diamond'; 'The Givens.'* The Yale Review: *'The Shades of Grand Central'; 'Word Silence.' 'The Cut' won the* New England Review/Bread Loaf Quarterly *Narrative Poetry Competition, 1989. The quotation on the last page is taken from* Beyond the Pleasure Principle, *translated by C. J. M. Hubback (New York: Boni & Liveright, 1924), p. 50.*

Perdido

Why All Good Music Is Sad

Before I knew that I would die,
I lolled in the cool green twilight
over the reef, the hot sun on my back,
watching the iridescent schools
flick and glide among stone flowers,
and the lacy fans blow back and forth
in the watery winds of the underworld.
I saw the long, bright muscle of a fish
writhing on a spear, spasm and flash,
a music violent and gleaming,
abandoned to its one desire.
The white radiance of Perdido
filtered down through the rocking gloom
so that it was Perdido there too,
in that strange, stroking, half-lit world.
Before I knew that love
would end my willful ignorance of death,
I didn't think there was much
left in me that was virgin, but there was.
That's why all good music is sad.
It makes the sound of the end before the end,
and leaves behind it
the ghost of the part that was sacrificed,
a chord to represent the membrane,
broken only once, that keeps the world away.
That's how the fish became the metaphor:
one lithe and silvery life impaled,
fighting death with its own failing beauty,

thrashing on the apex of its fear.
Art was once my cold solace,
the ice pack I held to love's torn body,
but that was before I lay
as if asleep above the wavering reef,
or saw the barbed spear strike the fish
that seemed for an instant to be
something outside myself, before I knew
that the sea was my bed and the fish was me.

A Minor Crush of Cells

I thought that the earth
would be the last thing that I loved,
the first and the last,

but there were many loves beyond it,

things I did not at first
know that I loved.

Children, for example,
though they no longer had much gravity,

would come sometimes
out onto the dusty, twilit sidewalks
to play their eternal games.

I remember the chalk's soft scraping.

It's not nostalgia, this hybrid sadness,
not the fragile boat that rides

the swift indwelling currents
into worlds that exclude
the loved things from each previous world,

though like nostalgia its halves
are always enemies, in this case
sex and death.

I look up into the night's faint green,
up into the pierced smoke of heaven,
and am for a moment

nothing but a minor crush of cells,

a bit of human substance
playful in imaginary forms.

Gravity draws down to me a halo
whipped up of holy dust

or dust from outer space:
dim chalk of moonlight, phosphor,

youth in the eyes of my former selves.

The Givens

One side of the dialogue
I have by heart,
but learned it so long ago
each phrase seems
sullenly dangerous now, in that
it withholds something I once knew.
The words go forth,
sleek pigeons into the wild sky,
smaller and smaller and smaller,
like pictures trapped in a telescope,
shrinking it-ward segment by segment.

I had as a child a mind
already rife with sacred greens
I could neither harvest nor ignore.
They sprang up everywhere:
from the black dirt of memory—
the old farm, its raspberries
diamonded with dew, etc.—
even from bodiless fantasy,
and from the mailbox full of letters
standing in for the various
emotions and kinds of news.

Part of myself must have
courted and married another part.
I don't know when it happened.
I know I heard both voices early on.

But one now drags its half of the duet
off into a scary song about
its intimations of the time ahead:
love, lost love, and love again,
and I dislike the long-drawn,
melancholy music that it makes.

But it's beautiful here
in this house above the valley,
close to the crumpled
paper of the clouds.
Birds return from invisible worlds.
Their feet print words on my sills.
And words weigh down the long,
soft-spoken branches of the evergreens,
weigh the unpruned
branches of abandoned orchards
down into the blond grass
where the pears,
grown small and hard with wildness,
soften and disappear.

And yet,
sometimes sick of the orderly,
pallid little stars,
I hear the stray heart's careless noise,
its tears and mysteries of laughter
close outside. It calls to me,
that voice, its ragged sweetness
intimate with everything I fear.

Worldliness

When I close my eyes,
the wind upbraids the dusk and snow
outside our room, fifteen floors
above the frozen park. Drink in hand,
he lies back in an open robe,
changing the channels by remote control.
The hotel's heating system blurts
sporadic clouds into the faint
geometry of unlit monoliths
beyond a flimsy Spanish balcony.
That, of all things, is what I see.

When the story finally ends,
the stray heart wanders home
to twitch in its sleep before the fire,
rummaging again through all the secret
rooms in which it was powerful and whole,
circling and circling its one conclusion,
which is not the story's conclusion.
So that now, elsewhere,
in harmless, flowering weather,
I wake in a steep-sided daydream
as a swimmer wakes in a wave.

*

I said, Men dream, but they go home.
Did that make me the devil,

me with my small-scale recklessness?
It was easy to see what he wanted:
the violent litheness of the young,

their mother-deafness.
When I spoke I think he heard
some of the sad music of his youth.
The car that loved the streets
of adolescence, the first wife

darkening in Italy among stone
fountains, ruins, historic flowers.
He was so . . . impermanent,
my newly made, my middle-aged roué,
my randy dreamer sliding through

a foxtrot cheek to cheek with alcohol.
I knew we could not go on sleeping forever
in the thin tent of the present tense,
and that the ink would someday feather away
from these words as if bent on escape.

I knew, and yet I lay down
in the sanctuary of the intellect
and took off my clothes there.
How could he deny me? He wanted
to change his life in my body.

*

The flip side of a wish is a fear,
and that was why we crushed
the heaven from those darkened rooms.

How easily the stubborn pearl
hoarded up and gave away
its infinite concentric mysteries,

how easily, how many times,
the nipples tightening, the mouth
wet muscle in the intimate marine.

We rode for a brief time
the salty violet undertow,
able to will the drowning we desired,

a liquid slide over the world's brink
in a rush of holy tremblings.
Once, undone by the threshing beauty

of our bodies, I imagined myself suddenly
naked in the restless cold cascades
of Taylor's Flume in the moonlight,

slipping with all my boy cousins
down through the bolts of darkness,
the waterfall loud and the rocks clean,

working our way against the muscular
currents, chased by the half-fear,
new to us then, for which I would

someday risk my accumulated self.
We swam as though the future
flowed around us, clean and cold,

but that was childhood—
pure, implacable, and long ago.
I meet him there, in the past,

where there are other names
for the heart in love with the arrow,
names for the spirit in the white pulse.

I go back, I meet him there,
whatever he asks me to do, I do.
I close my eyes,

and taste the cloudy caviar,
and hear outside whatever hotel
the metrically stupid traffic.

*

I want to love the story of my life,
the stories. Then I shall seem
not so much a creature in an index
of adventures or of dreams

as an interactive force that fed itself
on love, a force that did not atrophy.
And if it was reckless,
what will it matter?

I did what I did
for the sake of intensity,
and I am unrepentant
even in my emptiness.

*

Once, when I slipped in my robe
down the hotel corridor
to the ice machine at 2 a.m.,

what I thought was a boy
turned, his bucket full of glassy cubes,

but instead it was a half-sized man,
stopped in the face and chest,
his day's beard a blue rasp.

I saw us in the plate glass,
behind which snow was falling.

He backed me up against the ice machine

and pressed his unimaginable little
torso against me, but his heart beat so
anonymously hard that I forgave him.

Dream of the Interior

A dog that has been sleeping on a crypt
rouses and stands up, her yellow hide

sunken over the haunches,
pendant teats crusted and dry.

Green spotted lizards drop noisily
down through the serrated leaves,

rustling among the wooden crosses,
plastic flowers, and melted votive stubs,

the heaped sand bordered by shells.
What do I long for or deny such that

I dream up this paradise for myself,
and why is there so much death in it,

so many nameless grave-dunes?
Beyond the tumbled coral wall,

the heavy sea-grapes hang in dust,
the sea folds up its white rags

and shakes them out again,
and the crude oars of the fishermen

dip and rise and fling away
their sapphire droplets.

If I leave this place, could I find my way
home through the streets of sand,

the bones asleep in the heat?
A vine like honeysuckle scribbles

over the wall, one sweet taste
on the pale green tip of each stigma,

the delicately splayed petals spilling
pale orange dust and perfume.

If I put my tongue to a single flower,
I'd suspend here forever

in my unknown need,
swaying like the black dog

on his yellow bride, slightly off balance
among the dead, locked in a dream.

The Mistress

Crushed from the north
and west, where he is,
this filtering snow
amounts to longing,
distance being
a formal element at heart,
highlight of dust
in the green-black pines.

A camera cuts to nothing
whatever happened
and to whom,
cuts its subject
down to the fierce connectives,
tissue of light and dark,
the residue.

The snow will be my camera,
trapping in its acres
of sparkling synapses
whatever's left of the heat.

Then a sharp shadow from my life
will venture out
into the grainy fields
without desire—
gray bird or icicle,
branch lit by a simple white.

Not the snow that he brushed
bare-handed from his car
two days ago,
but a premonition of it.

A Whole Year of Love

Minnows glittered in the shallows,
a school of compass needles
fixed on a single dream.
Maybe the dream was hunger,
or a larger fish
concealed in the river like a knife,
and it was his hunger that turned them.
They flashed and vanished,

flashed and reappeared.
Late in the afternoon, rain
deepened the river in the ear.
I was standing on a porch I dreamed
or a porch in the past
(I can't remember which,
since each casts shadows on the other)
looking out over a wet green wilderness,
a landscape abridged by the peculiar way
the brain has of sidestepping the actual,
just as a whole year of love, for example,
might shrink to a stack of pale-colored,
just-laundered shirts. An image.

Above me, the mountains broke
from heavy cloud, shadowy and green
as the underside of the river
in which I swam, sometimes upstream,

sometimes downstream toward the knife,
its patient silver
thinning on the whetstone of the water.

Window in the Shape of a Diamond

Our room in the hotel was dark
except for a narrow slash of afternoon
containing a twig of orange leaves,
an empty field, and far away,
mountains in a pitch-blue sky.
Hour upon hour we lay,
the sheets kicked free,
watching the little landscape flare
in final colors of foreclosure,
as perfectly displaced
as the delicately tinted paper scenes
inside the hollow sugar eggs
that kids devour at Easter.
Beloved is a word concealing
four sharp points,
four kinds of innocence,
four winds of change.
One look inside it
and the world abruptly petrifies
into another of its
small cold monuments.

Lapses of Turquoise Sea

I bit down on the hard
rubber mouthpiece of the snorkel

and closed my eyes inside the oval glass,

closed them against
the foamy black transition,
the back-suck and momentary fear,

the pain of his name,

and when I opened them beneath
the turbulent blue wilderness,
uncountable two-dimensional fish

sliced slantways,
black-barred through the liquid salt.

Lacy corals looked too pliable to trail
red smoke of blood from each touch,

but they were hardened flames.

Every beauty was dangerous.

The water loved me. It wrestled
to keep me one with it. It dragged
and sighed and then forgot me

as I staggered, ludicrous in flippers,
back up into gravity.

Goodbye, stink of today's casualties:

the thirsty holes, the ruined shells,
the crab gone numb in the sun,

slick plants torn from deep beds,
now the late afternoon's fistful of scent

crushed and held to the nose to stand in
for the present, which in this place
is not a tense at all, but merely

the damp weight of a towel,
the pumice of hot sand.

Here at the Hotel Inviolable,

someone has brought a tray
of ice-clouded glasses and fruit
to the stone terrace:

fillets of orange melon veined with red.

Then night's unownable perfume.
The palms go on sharpening
their long, invisible blades,

and the sea erasing its infinity of names.

The evening's menu: one fish, one meat.
Guests come to dinner
dressed in imaginary lives.

Neither the candles nor the flowers
nor the muted crashing has a history.

Shadows of waiters trespass among us,
creatures of the magnifying night.

What follows a dog's exploratory bark?

All the ocean's lunging self-contained,
a sound within a sound:
wild, tumultuous, but small.

It's the sound inside the ear,
the always-sound,
but deeper now, sea-stung.

Bon voyage, sleek taxis
bound for the airport and home.

Each guest leaves with a corsage
still cold from the icebox,
petals of sea-froth

that will go on chilling,

stinging in the part of the memory
given to lapses of turquoise sea.

The Shades of Grand Central

You could tell that the flowers
splayed in the vendor's buckets

had come from the hothouse factories

lit all night to force more blooms.
Among the blue and scarlet flames
the eyes of the homeless flicked

from no one to no one,
and the name for them came to me
sharp in the winter dark

as if it had always been a word.

I climbed the heavy stairs
up out of the pit that steams
and quakes with machine life,

past flowers for the lover
and the lonely self,

flowers for the longtime dead and for
the fresh-cut holes in the frozen hill,

and for all the children
locked out of the world,

including my own,
about whom I know nothing,

not even how many, not even their names,

which are like thin ice and do not bear
the weight of my wondering about them.

I came up into the purifying cold,

the small, stinging arrows of snow,
and when I turned my head against it

I saw the hulk of a dumpster
out back of a rib house, in an alley.
A man in a hooded burlap robe

had led his flock of vagrant dogs to food.

What is an individual grief
but a flake in the storm?

He threw to the dogs the gnawed-on ribs
the restaurant had thrown away.

Snow diffused the harsh
halo of the streetlamp and lit
the folds of his strange apparel.

The dog bodies took each rib with a seizure,
white-backed and ravenous.

One Physics

Once, in the creaking hammock
late in summer, the afternoon
and evening overlapping,
I dreamed the structure of the self.
It had a queer, disorderly geometry
something like the atom's,
designed to be interactive.
But with what? It floated alone
on its gridwork. It had no mate.
When I awoke,
the mountains were barely upholding
the blue-green end of the spectrum,
about to be wet down
with royal lights. They looked
farther away than was possible,
and of a substance not of my world,
so that the flash of love
I felt for them seemed
purer than an earthly love,
and therefore surely counterfeit.
Why then did I dwell so long
on that failing violet light
as if I were one mind
with it, one physics?
And why did I compare it
to that other love, the human one,
the one that is only a man?
My house was falling into darkness

and the color in the distance seemed
a presence I could look at steadily
and it back out at me
as if we were cousins, maybe,
of different gists and yet
respectful of one another,
curious and unarmed. Scouts.
When the view from the porch
at last went under,
the thought that was broken in two
as the connection between me
and the purple mountain was broken
was this one, a wish:
that the atom-self, when it is lonely,
be consoled by such random couplings,
that it go on straying from wedding
to wedding, its delicate inner chaos
in effect its private parts.

In the Exploded View

the overlapping worlds
come all the way apart.
In the chill of first light
two boys rear up on the
back wheels of their bicycles,
swearing softly to one another
on their way to church.
They carry their choir robes,
still in the dry cleaner's plastic,
bunched over their handlebars.
The two worlds:
what we know and what we don't.
The here and now versus
the elsewhere and later.
The boys go ticking past me,
their wheels invisible,
the shock of potholes
in their skinny arms.
I remember the ecstasies
of the body, every one.
They are the streetlamps
I follow back into the mystery
that disappeared around me—
the cities of cloud,
the transient towers—
back to a street
with trees in cloudy bloom

where I stand, a shadow
on a bridge built of shadow,
and the fluty voices of the boys
pour out their cold Latin to the dawn.

Useless Islands

I'm trying to remember
what happened when love overtook me,

how the old self slipped
from its hard boundaries

like a ripe plum out of its skin.
It's a personal mystery.

It was August, each moment
setting fire to the next,

the woods already
bloodied by the first bright deaths.

I'm trying to remember, but there's
a blacked-out part to the story,

a steep, crashing wall of seawater,
a long thrill of fear. I was dragged

in an undertow as if out of sleep,
and the blue-green light I swam toward

was this paradise of islands,
these green days spilled

across a vast mercurial blue.
We lie in a flood of white sand

under the broken prism of the sky,
watching its fragile rays disappear

down the secretive avenues of palms.
How long can we lie here?

The luminous charcoal and manila clouds
cross like fish overhead.

His hand sleeps on my thigh.
The ratcheted voices of the tree frogs

start up their random music,
and we lie listening. It's a way

of passing more slowly through,
of dragging a stick in the water

like a brake. There's the dull
clop of goats on the red dirt road,

and the lisp of the sand beneath us.
What the leaves were saying

back in the other life,
the palms are saying here.

It's the words to the long slow sad
familiar hymn about the hourglass.

I lie beside my love
in the silence between two waves,

the grains of my body pouring.
I know that the second wave will ripen

and fall. It will fall in a world
that is emerald and sapphire,

lit by the sparks of the sea. A world
that will darken and abandon me.

The Condom Tree

Pleasure must slip
right through memory's barbed wire,
because sex makes lost things reappear.
This afternoon when I shut my eyes
beneath his body's heavy braille,
I fell through the rosy darkness
all the way back to my tenth year,
the year of the secret
place by the river,
where the old dam spilled
long ropes of water and the froth
chafed the small stones smooth.
I looked up and there it was,
a young maple
still raw in early spring,
and drooping pale
from every reachable branch
dozens of latex blooms.
I knew what they were,
that the older kids
had hung them there,
but the tree—was it beautiful,
caught in that dirty floral light,
or was it an ugly thing?
Beautiful first, and ugly afterward,
when I saw up close
the shriveled human skins?
That must be right,

though in the remembering
its value has been changed again,
and now that flowering
dapples the two of us
with its tendered shadows,
dapples the rumpled bed as it slips
out of the damp present
into our separate pasts.

Six Belons

The ruckled lips gaped slightly, but when
I slipped the knife in next to the hinge,
they closed to a stone.
The violence it took to unlock them!
Each wounded thing lay in opalescent milk
like an albino heart,
muscle sliced from the roof-shell.
I took each one pale and harmless
into my mouth and held it there,
tasting the difference between
the ligament and the pure, faintly
coffee-colored flesh that was unflinching
even in the acid of lemon juice,
so that I felt I was eating
not the body but the life in the body.
Afterward my mouth stayed greedy
though it carried the sea-rankness
away with it, a taste usually transient,
held for a moment beyond its time
on mustache or fingertip.
The shells looked abruptly old,
crudely fluted, gray-green, flecked
with the undersea equivalent of lichens,
and pearly, slick, bereft of all their meat.
The creatures themselves were gone,
the succulent indecent briny ghosts
that caused this arousal, this feeding,
and now a sudden loneliness.

The Cut

I had a sorrow that misled me.

Because we were childless,
I had, out of some sovereign,
stupid longing in my body,

invented a ghost-child,
a third person,

like a fruit neither male nor female,
its face a pale merger of his and mine.

We'd lie in the imaginary dark,
and the furled shape would slowly
open in the space still cooling between us,

a swirl of bluish shadow I could almost see,

and it would linger briefly there
attracted by the scent of love
until it strayed off into the pine wind,

or into the sound the brook makes under ice,
the seconds rushing past.

I comforted myself with the ironic
crux of an idea:

since life derives from a mated speck,
male and female alone at last
in the private heaven of a cell,

then all flesh must retain
some trace of its parenthood,

some faint androgyny that might
allow the mind to bear

both son and daughter,
both kinds of flower on a single stem.

The idea was a tourniquet,
an image of wholeness, though even

the cellular snow seemed genderless,

a zillion empty rooms,
a brilliant tide

on which our house rode
trailing woodsmoke, its windows
harshly sparked with distant sun.

*

We went back to Perdido by the sea.

It was raining, off-season,
and the small towns
were drowning in vacancy:

the miles of scrubbing palms,
the names of the hotels
scoured vague by sand.

The waves were still telling
the story we had come back to hear,

a story of erosion,
of how each life is cut into its shape
by the knife of diminishment:

the carved, forsaken beaches,
knife of the wind in the undulant grass.

The place was simultaneously
our only history and another history.

Not someone else's, but another
version of our own, and in that telling

there was no infant refugee to trespass
in the kingdom of our solitude.

What is it the waves erase?

Last year's sadness,
to make room for this year's?

I remember the sound of the sea
stealing back its souvenirs,

its hissing aphasia,
its spume and meringue,

all the defensive petals
loosening and falling away,
exposing the sound at its very center,

the one syllable, the *no*.

Feet slowed by seaweed, we walked
on a beach strewn with striped shells,

each one newborn and delicately
carved inside its rosy lip
with a set of dates.

He held one out to me,
but all I saw

was his finger, the fresh cut,

the stitches' exactness,
row of faint commas,
a wavering white splice

like the delicate little seam
dividing the testicles.

All other lives were long ago
sliced away from this one,

this animal singled out from the herd,
the rope around its neck
tightening, secure.

The dying music of the word *Perdido*
played in the plangent sadness of the rain.

It was a self-obliterating place,
perfect for futile wishing, but had,

like moonlight or snow or the future,

a blankness that invited
something human to defile it:

the hotel room full of sea-noise,

the waves collapsing out of sight,
backsliding and collapsing,

and the liquid gleam
they seemed to generate,

the bed a pool in which we could
drown our unwanted pasts,
and from which I could see emerge

the two young ghosts of our known selves:

the boy in him shyly stepping forward
gray with snow, and the girl I once was
venturing out from the forest of denials.

*

I can see that I've kept this story
caged in the past tense

as though the present were a spectator
come to gaze at the wild thing up close,

but it's easy to lie with metaphor.

It wasn't the child that I wanted,
but the hole the child's absence made.

The ghost was a vapor, a distraction.

Sex had become a well
into which I could throw

the trash of all my sorrows,
not just that one.

My childhood lay wrecked at the bottom,

and his, and all our nights together,
even the nights of the future,
where death lives.

I wanted the present engorged

like an animal that must daily eat
many times its own weight
just to survive.

And I wanted this to happen
at a cellular level, and repeatedly,

in the tireless violence of pleasure,

so I'd never have to do without
anything I could imagine.

It was a potent greed that ruled in me,
a lust, a childish grabbiness
with sex as its locus.

*

Now the balsam-scented cold
pours into my dream,

dispersing its phantoms
back into unconsciousness,
and the snow

blown up off the crests of the drifts
ticks in the green needles

and in the last few leaves
grown metallic and abstract,

each one bearing
its tiny, meticulous dates.

The brook rushes on toward a deeper cold.

In its white noise I hear the clarities
swimming away from me, icy shadows,
as sleep comes on.

Sleep itself is a shadow,

a heavy, invisible wave that swells
and breaks over us where we lie

in the moonlight dried white on our sheets.

Chanel No. 5

Life had become a sort of gorgeous elegy,
intimate with things about to be lost.

The waiter's hand on the wineglass
seemed an intermediary flame,

the atoms rampant inside it,

though it moved slowly
and hesitated slightly
before it was withdrawn

as if it meant to ask
whether anything more was wanted.

Abstracted by the static of the surf,

I dined alone, the beach hotel
half empty in the off-season,

the honeymooning couple
at the table next to mine

caressing with their voices
the still-folded map of their future,

their two armies still in reserve,

the flowers massed between them
a flimsy barricade
against their wakening grief.

The long pin of her corsage
pierced the thin silk on her breast:
white flower, green leaf, black dress.

In her perfume I smelled
the residue of all their recent happiness,
a sweetness corrupted by the sea, and yet

she wore it innocently, that target.

It was a fledgling bitterness I caught
off a shred of air that had touched her dress
as she rose to follow her husband-mystery.

The little emblem inside the flame,
the male and female become one,

was blackening back in their room

overlooking the sea, but before they
hurried back to it, she looked at me,
and, as if to inoculate herself against me,

inclined her head to smell her own gardenia.

Remember Death

Nothing in the red leaves
distinguishes this year from any other.
The haunted planet could be sloughing off
its worn-out parts in any age,
spreading its musky bedding
under the trees for us to lie on.
I look up over his shoulder as he enters me,
up into the high vaults
of the Church of the Falling Leaf,
and hear the swollen hum, and see
not ten feet above us
the pale gray paper of the nest,
the branch bent down,
wasps dropping from the hole
like little paratroopers
then shooting sideways away.
The small sticks hurt my back
but not very much, not enough to rouse me
from the sweet slide in and out
which says, I'm here, I'm here,
I'm here in the river of stinging leaves.
And I'll be back—that gets said
in the slowness of the goodbye.

The Blade of Nostalgia

When fed into the crude, imaginary
machine we call the memory,

the brain's hard pictures
slide into the suggestive
waters of the counterfeit.

They come out glamorous and simplified,

even the violent ones,
even the ones that are snapshots of fear.

Maybe those costumed,
clung-to fragments are the first wedge

nostalgia drives into our dreaming.

Maybe our dreams are corrupted
right from the start: the weight

of apples in the blossoms overhead.

Even the two thin reddish dogs
nosing down the aisles of crippled trees,
digging in the weak shade

thrown by the first flowerers,

snuffle in the blackened leaves
for the scent of a dead year.

Childhood, first love, first loss of love—

the saying of their names
brings an ache to the teeth
like that of tears withheld.

What must happen now
is that the small funerals
celebrated in the left-behind life

for their black exotica, their high relief,

their candles and withered wreaths,
must be allowed to pass through
into the sleeping world,

there to be preserved and honored
in the fullness and color of their forms,

their past lives their coffins.

Goodbye then to all innocent surprise
at mortality's panache,
and goodbye to the children fallen

ahead of me into the slow whirlpool
I conceal within myself, my death,

into its snow-froth and the green-black
muscle of its persuasion.

The spirits of children
must look like the spirits of animals,
though in the adult human

the vacancy left by the child
probably darkens the surviving form.

The apples drop their blossom-shadows
onto the still-brown grass.
Old selves, this is partly for you,

there at the edge of the woods
like a troop of boy soldiers.

You can go on living with the blade
of nostalgia in your hearts forever,
my pale darlings. It changes nothing.

Don't you recognize me? I admit
I too am almost invisible now, almost.

Like everything else, I take on
light and color from outside myself,
but it is old light, old paint.

The first shadows are supple ones,
school of gray glimpses, insubstantial.

In children, the quality of darkness
changes inside the sleeping mouth,

and the ghost of child-grime—
that infinite smudge of no color—

blows off into the afterlife.

The Imaginary Land

A respectful hush-turned-to-silence
fell in a restaurant when a woman,
once a famous dancer,

entered the room in a split dress,
her surgical corseting thus displayed,

and in spite of her formalizing arthritis

managed in one gesture to suggest
the full range of her former gift—

willed it, a moment free of gravity—

as she flicked the pink
napkin from the table and sat,

so that afterward we wandered
joyfully home in the heavy starlight,

recklessly kissing alongside the stone wall

where the odorless rose of Sharon
explodes in the dark

and the camellias contradict themselves,
spoiling and blooming simultaneously,

and since we were ourselves
ambassadors of that perishable kingdom,

we went on holding hands,
went on whispering one night's
secrets into the opening flowers

in peace—peace, the imaginary land.

The Somersault

Just for the tarry smudge and hiss of sap
I struck a match in a mesh of twigs
the brook had thrust among the rocks.
Up in the big birches the smoke
thinned to a rippling intake of light
that was private, somehow, exclusive—
a fish visible a second in rough water,
jewels behind a limo's tinted glass.
Something was making a meaning up there,
some kindling intelligence
that made me feel excluded from the future,
that my mind would stop and its continue,
so that I wanted to be made of its gist
instead of my own, which was gravid and dim.
It seemed to me that each leaf shook
and each spark flew toward some
immaculate abstraction and away from
the smoky prison of the human world.
I wanted to track that black compression
to the end of consciousness, to curve my spine
back into the somersault begun so long ago,
the C-shape that slipped from sexual water
onto the warm lawns of childhood,
a childish grace now poised in the mind
like a jackknife, a grace that ends
in the sparks all around us,
rising and vanishing, changed to ash flecks.

Revenge

He was standing on the hotel balcony
when I awoke, watching the late afternoon

sluice down green-gold
over the fronds of the royal palms.

Palms in wind make a sound
like knives being sharpened,

languorous in my dispersing sleep,
slice-slicing against themselves.

He was watching the melon-colored light
run over the slow swells,

and the pleasure boats trailing
their long white creamy wakes,

their engines shuddering.
My waking thought was that

I was waking *inside a century*,
a cage bigger than our lives,

and that the freedom to roam around in it
was an illusion we both had, or an irony

we'd once abided by but had forgotten,
walking in the drifting dunes of light,

the snows of Perdido, snows of crushed coral,
on the edge of the trespassing sea.

The sheets were imprinted on my skin.
The cool air fingered each crease

and the fresh grass matting felt
pleasingly harsh and raw underfoot.

No one could see me
there in the palm shadows, naked

and dappled by the sun's warm camouflage.
The passing seconds were almost visible,

a faintly glamorous stream of light
that flowed over the moving boats,

brightened the frictional leaves.
He put his arm around my shoulders,

the smell of the day in his shirt,
so that his thumb not quite touched

my nipple, which shriveled,
and with the other hand slowly

unbuttoned and unzipped himself,
all the while watching the pleasure boats

glide past us trailing bits of broken mirror,
their engines pulsing steadily,

fueled by what's left of the future.

Word Silence

There's a flame like the flame of fucking
that longs to be put out: words are filings
drawn toward a vast magnetic silence.
The loins ask their usual question
concerning loneliness.
The answer is always a mountaintop
erasing itself in a cloud.
It's as if the mind keeps flipping
a coin with a lullaby on one side
and a frightening thrill on the other,
and if it lands it's
back in the air at once.
A word can rub itself rosy
against its cage of context,
starting a small fire in the sentence
and trapping for a moment
the twin scents of now and goodbye.
The sexual mimicry always surprises me:
the long dive the talky mind makes
into the pleasures of its native dark.
Like pain, such joy is locked
in forgetfulness, and the prisoner
must shout for freedom again and again.
Is that what breaks the sentences apart
and spreads their embers in a cooling silence?
The pen lies in the bleach of sunlight
fallen on the desk, ghost-sheet of a bed
turned back. If I look for a long time

into its wordlessness, I can see
the vestiges of something that I knew
dissolving. Something that I no longer know.
And there I sleep like an innocent
among the words I loved
but crushed for their inflammable perfumes.

O Miami

Wherever the cloth of my dress touched me
it seemed a hand was about to touch me.
The dark drew heat from my skin,
a mild sunburn that made the palm of my hand
itch in his, and my feet chafe
in the cool sugary sand, the wave-froth.
Miami weltered in the wakes of speedboats,
its lights pink-silver, smeared across the bay.
We paid two dollars to walk on the pier,
its long eroded sticky boards,
past the spigots and the crude scaling tables
to the end where a man shone a flashlight
into the tangled glitter of his tackle box.
Below us the water rocked and smashed.
I tugged the tails of his shirt
out of his pants and slipped both hands
up the ladder of his back,
for which he opened a look at me
that made the muscles of my body swim
like a school of quick fish, flinching as one,
rising to feed in water that was mirror-clean
and empty, deep, abstract.
Among them gleamed the bright hook,
the hook that drags death into the story,
the idea of death which starts so barbed and small.
The man laid a catfish out on the rough wood,
and pierced its skull with an awl.
Tore the lure from the gristly tissue of the lips.

Across the bay, the city spilled its languid neons.
His heart beat under my hand.
Every muscle was a fish in the shoal,
and every act from that point on
an act of defiance: his mouth on my throat,
my hand in his salty hair, so that
when he turned the key in the hotel room door
I was already stepping out of my sandals.
The maid had turned down the bed.
Every muscle was a fish. I heard my own voice
cry out *O Miami*, words he took from me.
The water-sound was loud in the palmy dark,
and the sound the fish made beating
the rough boards with its flagrant silver tail.
The hook sinks down through the dream of love.
The moment of greeting is the moment of farewell.

The Stolen Emblem

The spectral stripe
that clings to the winter horizon
is the iceblink.

It's the sun sent back
toward itself by the frozen world.

I flew into its cold mirage.

From that far,
the earth looked shrunken and pilfered,

bitten by cloud-shadows,
stung by shreds of wind.

I saw the blackened granite of a city
struck with pinkish fire,

the buildings hard-edged, flaring
as the twilight deepened—

a field of headstones
torched by remnant light.

It was an image of the planet
starved to its bones by the mind,
brightened and simplified,

like snow on the roof of a house
abandoned to evening, no one home.

When the mind fastens on something alien,

it sharpens to a cruel wind.
It finds the cracks.

That's how death gets in.

But when it tries to picture *itself*,
it slips with its twin into the mirror's
water-light, and together

they swim toward an imaginary shore.

So the image of the world arrived
contaminated in my eye,
contaminated by its history in me.

It was an emblem, an invention,
like the beating heart reduced

to a range of shivery
blue mountains on the screen.

Its meaning lay in my gloss on myself:

was I willing to track the image
back into the part of myself
where all the dead loves are stored,

the dead loves impacted like rubies
in the dark, still warm to the touch?

And willing or not, where was the door?

There's no coherent cosmology.
Only a series of secrets

slipped from one layer to another,
inner to outer.

The self hides in the center,
and the mind is what
crackles around it—its voice.

I loved the little globe,
its corrugations and blue foil.
Death got in when love got in.

Love, that leaves the door unlocked.

That was why the earth
had shrunken so,
why the house was cold though hopeful,

why the flowers lay clouded in cellophane—
they were for later.

I looked down and saw the sphere,
the astral light,

the tear sprouting in my eye.

Someone had placed
a transparency marked with knowledge
over the world, as if knowledge

were a sadness overlaid
on the small green islands in the sea,

the polar blankness, and the countries
overcast by fuming factories.

As if all this were revealed
on a dingy pull-down map

the teacher keeps poking with a stick.

I used to live inside
its lines and colors,
inside its body,

kicking up the weightless snow,
shivering in the gloom

the old pines cast down—
their bristling shadows—
and the small soundless glittering

of branches letting slip
their weight of white

in the softening sparkle of the sun.

No footprints in the picture,
no smoke. But now I saw
scrawled over the loved place

the names of the alien chemicals,
carbons and chlorides,

and the future generations of the fox—
the silver animal, the ghost dog—

dwindling into myth,
withdrawn into a place beneath the snow,

and the trout in the stream
finning away its allotment of hours.

But the emblem was not
a jewel of ecology.

It was a jewel—a fossil—of love.
Of sweetness perishing.

It's not the world (this stony hull,
this rampant garden) that dies,

that disappears inside the metaphor,
though it dies and disappears.

Here, inside, it's only a swirl of matter:
grapevine and flock-in-flight
and black tonnage of ocean depth

left to their wild commingling.

It's the extinction of the thinking mind,
the ink-dark paralysis, that terrifies,

that fascinates me here, that divorces
the self into its lonely parts.

It's the trembling reflection
we see in the face of another,

and the fact that it breaks
when we sleep
back into nothingness because

no one is left to name it.

So it's not the little mirrors
falling from the eyes, or the cane

tapping in the orange leaves
that undoes us,

but the disfigurement,
the shame of bearing all the ugly
signatures of our abandoned selves:

early versions of the voice
still stupid with logic,

the puckering scars, the badly worked
crude mine shafts to the heart.

It's the farewells that wear us out.
The funerals.

I remember the salt dark
I swam through to get here,

now the daughter of a daughter
of a daughter, daughter of atoms.

Atoms! Each one a window through which
the wilderness of the future leaks,

poor water blank as infancy.
But there's solace in that random spillage,

solace in the personal atomic breakdown.

The city burned,
and I felt in my cells a waywardness,

an anarchy that thrilled
to the fact that I will someday

drown in the spiraling storms.

I loved both material worlds,
the one I was
and the one surrounding me.

I was the living carting the dead around.
I was a treeful of rings.

I longed through the imaginary snow
for an altar outside myself.

I wanted each extinction
dignified with flowers,

candles all around it
spilling hot rivulets of wax.

Love made the violence in my cells.

It made of itself a knife and scraped away
the dust and the trash.
In short, the past.

What else was lost, and where did it go?
Who has it now, and will I recognize
myself when I am mirror to myself?

The questions turn on themselves
mid-asking, and diminish.

I diminish, shucking my skins as I go.

And just as the metaphor steals
the meaning for itself,

I steal the emblem.

Poor world of tinder.
Poor fuel to which I hold

the flame of my invention.

Is every life an elegy?
Unto itself. I answer myself.

There are only two tenses,
the flame and the ashes.

Time is the only verb.

*Thus these reproductive cells
operate against the death of the
living substance and are able to
win for it what must seem to
us to be potential immortality,
although perhaps it only means a
lengthening of the path to death.*

—*Freud*

*

For Russell Banks